The Beaded Lampshade Book

TRADING & PUBLISHING COMPANY

LA MESA, CALIFORNIA

ISBN 0-9645957-1-0
Library of Congress Catalog Card Number: 95-95201
San: 298-5829

All illustrations by Wendy Simpson Conner
Photography by Don Brandos
Printed proudly in the United States of America

FIRST PRINTING: NOVEMBER, 1995

ACKNOWLEDGMENTS:

*To Jennie, Joni, Paul, Steve, Priscilla,
and everyone who bought and loved*
The Best Little Beading Book.

Introduction

Beaded lampshades can be such a wonderful addition to your home or studio. They can add to the drama of the room, and create an atmosphere all their own. The designs are so varied, and the colors are endless, that you can literally redesign a room around a new lampshade.

My grandmother, Jennie, who designed jewelry for the Ziegfeld Follies, also designed beaded lampshades. We have many of her beautiful old designs. Beaded lampshades were all the rage in those days — if you ever go into an antique shop, you'll be amazed at the complexity of these old lampshades.

I've taken some of my grandmother's designs and adapted them, using today's materials. There are thirteen designs for lampshades in this book. They range from the very intricate (not for the faint-of-heart) to the very, VERY easy (my seven year old could do them). Some require stitching, some work up on wire, and there's even one that utilizes cement — quite a range!

As with my other books, there are a lot of diagrams, because most people are visually-oriented, and learn best from step-by-step instructions. As with everything I do, I tend to be a bit obsessive-compulsive, so this book is as chock-full of ideas as my others. I do recommend reading *The Best Little Beading Book* (by me) as a backup to this book, as there's a lot of background information that could be helpful in there.

These books are the beginning of a series of 25 books on beads and beading techniques, to be published in the next three years.

I hope you enjoy *The Beaded Lampshade Book*, and find these projects fun.

As always, I love hearing your wonderful comments. Please feel free to write me c/o The Interstellar Trading and Publishing Company, Post Office Box 2215, La Mesa, California, 91943.

Happy Beading!

"Me"

Table of Contents

Types of Beads

Heaven knows there's a *planet* full of beads out there! How do you know which type will work best for your lampshades?

When working on a project like a lampshade, it's very important that your beads be uniform in size (so there are no deviations in your design); that the beads be colorfast and lightfast (there's nothing worse than spending three weeks on a project, only to have it fade in one day); and well-made so that they last.

I recommend using transparent or translucent glass or crystal.

Glass beads made in the Czech Republic are the best beads in the world. The tradition of making beads is centuries old there . . . they have perfected it to an art! The variety is endless . . . from specialty beads to foil beads to seedbeads to bugle beads to fire-polished crystal to pressed glass . . . every type of bead you can imagine. When you see the variety available, you will salivate! They are easily available, and there are literally *millions* of variations.

Beads from the Czech Republic are the only ones I know of that give you the high quality that you need, plus are a very good value for the money.

Some beads that come from other countries may not give you the quality that lampshades demand. If you choose to use these other beads, you may need to sort them for size, and test for colorfastness.

The worst beads to fade are called "lined beads", which is a type of seedbead. These have a fairly transparent outer layer of glass covering an inner layer of glass in a different color. Because of this process of layering, many times these beads will fade (if the layers have been incorrectly applied). To see if a bead may fade, thread a needle with thread, then dip the thread in alcohol. Run this needle and thread through the bead. If the color comes off, then it will fade.

Another problem is with metallic-looking seedbeads. Sometimes, just the chemical reaction of being touched by your hands will remove the outer metallic layer, leaving you with a yucky, dull uninteresting bead. To test if the finish is stable, try holding a small bunch of beads in the palm of your hand for about two minutes. If the color comes off, don't use them.

A way to test for lightfastness is to set the beads on the windowsill in direct sunlight for a day or so. Then, compare them to beads from the same hank. Are they still the same color? If not, then you know what to expect as time goes on.

Some beads may not hold up next to the heat of a lightbulb. Be careful of beads that look like two halves of different color beads have been fused together. Sometimes, the temperatures of the two colors of glass cools or heats at a different rate, and then you have the beads "popping" apart.

I very rarely use plastic beads (although there is one design in the book that does use plastic). Plastic is duller than glass, and the light doesn't pass through the bead with the same "zip" that glass has. Plastic is cheaper, but I feel it is truly inferior when it comes to making lampshades. Some of the newer acrylics might be clearer and look nicer, and for a child's room they may be an (unbreakable) option that you may wish to use. Choose wisely — steer clear of anything that has badly-finished seams.

In the end, the quality of your beads will only enhance your own beautiful craftsmanship. If you start out with the best, then you will have a treasure that will become a family heirloom.

Bugle Beads

Bugle beads are measured by their lengths. Most are made to be compatible with a size 11/0 seedbead's diameter. Sometimes you will find other diameters in bugle beads, but this is considered unusual. Longer bugle beads are measured by millimeters, shorter ones by the table below. They can be straight, or twisted. They come in many finishes.

The sizing for bugles seems to roughly correspond to eighths of an inch. (a size five bugle is very close to 5/8's of an inch in length; a size four is about 4/8", etc.) The larger sizes are usually referred to by their length in millimeters (a size 20 would be 20mm long). The shorter lengths are shown below.

| ½ | 1 | 2 | 3 | 4 | 5 |

Seed Beads

Very small beads are called seedbeads. They come in different sizes and finishes, and require smaller, finer needles and thread. They work well for lampshades, because they fill in the gaps and help your pattern to hang better. They're terrific when making a charted design (please see the butterfly pattern) — because of their size, you can get a lot of detail into a small area.

Seedbeads are measured by a very unusual method. They're not sized like other beads; sizing is based on the size of the rods used for making the glass beads (measured in increments called "aughts", which are roughly equivalent to ½ centimeter. Aught means 0). The smaller the number, the larger the bead. Thus, 11/0 is smaller than 7/0. What this really means is 11x0, versus 7x0 (sort of on a negative scale). Like in electronics, higher multiples of aught are actually smaller than lower multiples of aught. Pretty confusing, huh? To further complicate matters, each country that produces these beads has a different sizing system, so a Czech 11/0 may differ slightly from a Japanese 11/0. The chart on the right is based on Czech sizing.

For making beaded lampshades, I recommend using a size 11/0 or larger. Otherwise, you will have a project that will last you well into the next millineum.

	16/0
	15/0
	14/0
	13/0
	12/0
	11/0
	10/0
	9/0
	8/0
	7/0
	6/0
	5/0
	4/0
	3/0
	2/0
	1/0

Some descriptions you may hear about seedbeads are:

BUGLE BEADS - Long, tube shaped beads available in several lengths (see above).

CARNIVAL GLASS - brightly colored clear glass beads, made in the early part of the century.

CEYLON - Also called "pearl", has a glossy, creamy ("pearlized") finish.

CHALKWHITE - Dull finish, white opaque seedbeads.

CHARLOTTE BEAD - Traditionally used in Native American beadwork, a size 13/0 opaque seed bead that is cut and faceted like crystal. (very difficult to find).

"E" BEAD - A size 6/0 bead.

FROST - Frosted finish

HEXAGON-CUT - Bead cut with 6 sides; reflects light.

INDIAN BEAD - An opaque "pony" bead.

IRIS - Transluscent, glossy appearance.

LINED - Color inside a bead with a clear or tinted surface outside (sometimes not too colorfast)

LUSTRE - Has a very glassy, "bright" quality

METALLIC - Has a metallic finish, available in traditional metal colors (gold, bronze, silver), and also other bright colors.

OPAQUE LUSTRE - Glossy, deep color

OPAQUE DYED - Opaque, but with a muted, almost "watercolor" look; sometimes not completely colorfast.

RAINBOW - Bright, clear, vivid colors (carnival glass)

ROCAILLE - Silver or gold lined, with square holes.

SILKY CUT - Satiny, silky finish. Also known as *"SATIN"*.

THREE-CUT - Highly reflective bead, with three surfaces showing at one time. This really catches the light. Used often on clothing.

TILE CUT - A very squared cyllindrical bead that weaves well due to its uniformity (like a short bugle bead.

TRANSLUCENT - "French Opal"

TRANSPARENT - clear glass

TWO-CUT - Reflective bead, with two surfaces showing at one time.

WHITE HEART BEADS - Beads of a deep color on the outside with white "chalky" centers. Usually found with deep red coloring.

You'll get the most dramatic effects when using beads that the light can pass through. When shopping for your beads, hold them up to the light to see what they look like when lit from the rear.

Stringing Media

When making a lampshade, one of your highest priorities in choosing a stringing medium is how to know what will last.

There are so many factors that can damage your lampshade: light, dust, rapid temperature deviations (caused by the repeated heating and cooling of the lightbulb), and just time itself taking a toll. How do you know what to use?

The first question to ask yourself is which beads you are using for your project. This will help to govern which stringing media is most appropriate.

The golden rule when picking a stringing medium is to try to fill the holes in the bead as full as possible to reduce friction. If you have a large heavy bead and you use a wimpy little thread, you can bet it will break sooner than later.

When using seedbeads, you can use **NYMO,** which is a nylon thread similar in consistency to dental floss, but definitely stronger and meant to last. This is not intended for really heavy beads, but will work with your seedbeads. It comes in many sizes, but I recommend only using "D" or "F" for your lampshades. Whenever possible, always work with your thread doubled for extra strength.

When using larger beads, you can use **NYLON BEAD CORD** or **SILK THREAD** (preferrably on spools) in the "F" weight. If the holes in your beads are slightly smaller, then you could use "D" or "E". These two media use the same calibration system, and are pretty much interchangable. It is important to work as tightly as you can, otherwise you may experience stretching in your threads later on. Again, work with your thread doubled. Try to match the color of your beads to your thread, otherwise if the thread is too dark, it will be too shocking against the beads; if it's too light, it will look cheap.

It is also possible to use **TIGER TAIL,** which is the nickname for a nylon-coated wire cable. It's used for heavy or sharp beads (i.e., crystal that might cut silk). Used in conjunction with crimp beads, which have little "teeth" inside, it's a nice, strong, quick way to make a lampshade.

You can also use **20** or **24 GAUGE WIRE** (please see gold and fuschia lampshade), and simply wirebend the shade.

The possibilities are endless. The main things to be sure of is that the medium doesn't stretch too much (avoid dacron and some synthetics — too much stretch), and that it doesn't rot (avoid cotton — it usually rots). Stay away from nylon filament (fishing line), because it is very heat reactive and will crack and break. Also . . . make sure that whatever you use isn't going to touch the lightbulb, and it should NEVER be made of anything potentially flammable!

Needles

When making a lampshade, your needle is half the battle! With the right tools, your work will run much smoother. A good, strong, stiff, thin needle is very important. Don't use the flexible twisted wire needles for this . . . you will become frustrated very easily because it's not moving along fast enough. Below are the needles that will help speed up the work on your lampshade.

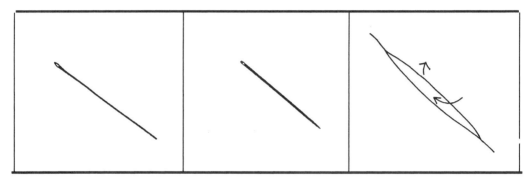

ENGLISH BEADING NEEDLES

The smaller the needle, the larger the number. Calibrated to work with seedbeads; A #10 needle works with a #10 seed bead.

SHARPS

Great for beading on fabric or plastic lampshades; Fairly fine with small round eyes; good and strong. Comes in different sizes.

LARGE-EYED NEEDLES

Virtually the entire needle is the eye - it's super-easy to thread! Just twist and thread, then untwist and it will "grab" your thread and hold it in place. Works best with larger beads, it's great for "scooping" and stringing a lot of beads at one time.

Glues / Cements

Most of the lampshades in this book require using a thread-type stringing medium, which requires cementing your knots whenever possible. One of the lampshades requires a good strong cement for adhering the beads right onto the fabric shade. You'll use different cements for each application.

WATCH MAKER'S CEMENT

Watch Makers' Cement is different from regular cement because the "grain" of it seems smaller — it seems to soak in better for fine work. Being a cement, it does penetrate what it is bonding. It's ideal for cementing the knots in your threads as you need to with your lampshade. It's NOT strong enough for a heavy-duty bond. It has a tiny little applicator tip, so it doesn't glop everywhere when you use it. It makes a bond that is rigid. Drying time is about 5 minutes.

CRAFTERS' CEMENT

This is the cement you find in craft stores. The applicators are usually not really fine, and sometimes you need to apply (sparingly) with a toothpick. If it dries with a lot of excess, you will see it and not be able to remove it. This has more "bite" than the previous cement, and is ideal for cementing beads onto fabric lampshades. It will give you a nice, industrial strength bond. Drying times differ from brand to brand, from 5 minutes to 24 hours, depending on your use. The thicker the cemented area, the longer it will take to dry.

• • •

Don't use any adhesive that is dependent on heat (like a "hot" glue gun) — the minute it cools or heats, it could unglue what you have put together.

Also, please be careful with whatever adhesive you choose. Some are quite flammable. You'll need to read and follow the product directions printed on the package. Common sense should prevail. Never adhere anything to a lightbulb or surface that will get too hot, and always have adequate ventilation when working with cements.

Fringing Styles

There are so many ways to make a fringe! It's not just that straight up-and-down that you'd expect — as you can see, there are lots of variations.

A simple fringe with one pivot bead at the bottom.

The same fringe, but with 3 or 5 pivot beads.

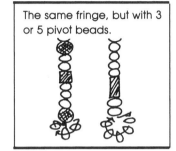

Make loops instead of pivot beads

Instead of fringe, make loops that cascade across

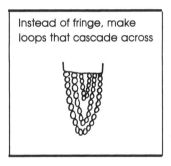

Mix your loops with fringe

Add charms to the bottom of your fringe.

Make your fringe bottoms in a chevron pattern.

One fringe can attach to another by joining them at the bottom.

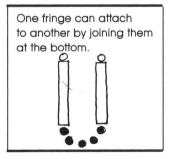

Fringe bottoms can be all one length, or random

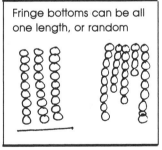

Try modifying some of the designs in this book by mixing fringing styles

AT LEFT:
Comanche Stitch & Turkish Lampshades

PREVIOUS PAGE:
Woven African Lampshade

FRONT COVER:
Art Deco Lampshade

AT RIGHT:
Diamond Stitch & Tiger Tail Lampshades

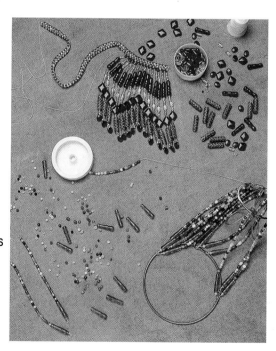

AT RIGHT:

Woven Mesh, Sewing Machine, &

     Peyote Stitch Lampshades

AT LEFT:
Cemented & Freeform Lampshades

NEXT PAGE:
Crystal & Wire Lampshade

BACK COVER:
Butterfly Lampshade

Types of Lampshade Frames

There are several types of frames to build your beadwork on.

1. The standard/cloth plastic frame

This wire frame is covered with a cloth outside/plastic liner inside. This is the standard that almost every lamp comes with. You can use one from an existing lamp, or you can purchase them anywhere — they're easy to find and inexpensive. They usually have wire loops at the top that clip onto your bulb (A), or a recessed ring that sits on the metal switch part of the lamp just below the bulb (B).

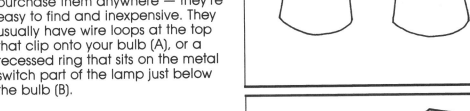

2. The flaired shade

This is pretty much a variation of number one, but the angle of the curve is more exaggerated (C). You'll also see this one in a squared version (D).

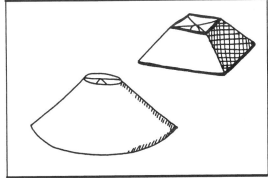

3. The plain wire frame

This consists of just the wire frame top with two loops for the lightbulb. You can almost make this out of coat hangers. You can purchase this at most decorator shops, or just take the fabric/plastic off of the previous frames.

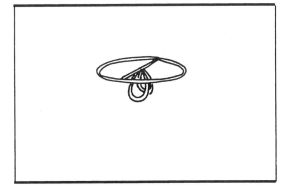

4. *The wire "cage"*

This one is usually used for fabric covering or stained glass — it has a wire structure that resembles a cage.

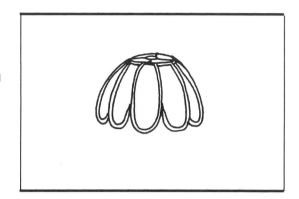

5. *The plastic dome*

These are very inexpensive, and look like upside-down plastic bowls. Most of them come with a finial on top (kind of like a hood ornament), which can be replaced by fancier ones that go better with your design.

6. *Enhancing storebought lampshades*

You can always buy a lamp that just cries out to be redesigned (like the black art deco one on the cover) and add a little something of your own to spruce it up.

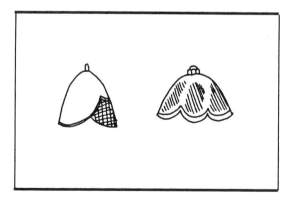

How to Measure Your Lampshade

Remember geometry? Remember how we hated circumferences, radaii, and PI? Well, it's a good thing we kept all those notes from seventh grade, 'cause we need them now!

Not every lampshade needs to be this exact, but if you're beading a fringe that has a pattern that has to be followed closely, this should help a lot!

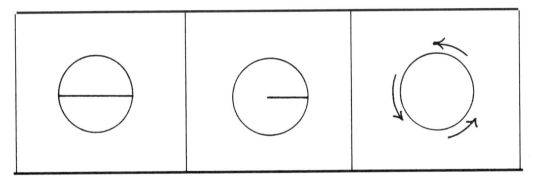

DIAMETER
The measurement from one side to the other of a circle is called the diameter

RADIUS
Half a diameter is a radius.

CIRCUMFERENCE
The measurement around the outside of the circle (the outline) is a circumference.

When beading a lampshade, the measurement of the circumference is what you'll need to know, because that's usually what you'll be beading.

Rather than struggling with the tape measure to get it to lie flat as you measure the circumference, why not use that old geometry?

CIRCUMFERENCE = THE DIAMETER x PI

PI is a Greek math thing that equals 3.14 when it's rounded off. This is the symbol of PI: π

So, if you buy a lampshade that's got a 10" diameter, just multiply that by PI (3.14) and you'll know that the circumference is 31.4".

This is the first step in making that lampshade. Now, you can adjust your pattern so that it will evenly fill the area you need to bead. You don't want to start your pattern and have it fall short or run over the circumference and overlap. A little planning at this stage can save you much nail biting later on.

Say that your pattern is 3" wide. You'll repeat it for a total of 10 times. But, you'd fall short of the circumerence of the lampshade by 1.4". Now you know you can adjust by adding a little space between each repeat of the pattern to fill it in properly.

To find out just how much you need to fill in, take your leftover space (1.4"), and divide by 10. You can say that you have 1 2/5" (fraction equivalent) or 7/5". You can either work out the rest of the math (good luck), or just rough it to say that you need to skip less than 1/5" between each repeat (about 1/6" is close enough), and lay out your pattern accordingly.

Now, this probably sounds like you need to be a physicist to make this lampshade, but that's not the case. If math is not your thing, you can buy a calculator that will work it all out for you (the math, not the lampshade)!

●●

Adjusting the Design to Fit the Lampshade

●●

You're going to have an easier job if you first start with the lampshade and then build the design to fit it, rather than making the beaded part, then driving all over town to find a shade or frame that will work.

If you are unable to find a lampshade in the dimensions that each project calls for, it's really not that hard to do a little math (see above) to alter your pattern so that it will fit. Even when the lampshade frame says it is a certain size, it is best to measure for yourself. Many times manufacturers will ballpark a size, and even 1/8" can sometimes alter the way your design comes together.

There are many unusual frames to be found; you can even wirebend your own unique frame out of coathangers.

What's really nice is that you can adapt some of these patterns and make matching window or door curtains (a beaded valance in a doorway looks so lovely).

Cemented Shades

Let's start with the easiest shade of all . . . you don't need math equations, you don't even need to know how to sew!

If you've ever visited Los Angeles, there is a truly unique place called the Watts Towers. It was created over many years, by simply cementing odds and ends of broken glass, pottery, dishes, bottles, and other items to wire armature. The end result is as startling as it is beautiful. It looks like something from another world, and it has a grace and beauty that catches you unaware. As you look among the treasures that have been brought together, a million questions come to mind. Assembling the unusual is a wonderful way to create beauty.

This lampshade is like that. Use your old beads, bits of broken dishes, sea shells, old broken jewelry, multicolor seedbeads, or whatever catches your fancy. Each one you make will be unique. This is a great rainy day project for children.

Supplies Needed:

- 527 cement
- One standard lampshade, appx. 5" high, with a 3" circumference at the top and a 5" circumference at the bottom
- One bag of misc. beads (appx. one pound), but this will differ by the beads and shade you choose.

Step One:

Work in small areas at a time. Squeeze on a moderate amount of cement to the outside of the lampshade, and lay the beads in it while it's still wet. You can work either randomly or in a pattern. Only use as much cement as you'll need at one time. Allow several hours to dry.

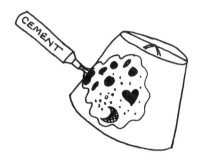

Step Two:

Build your design onto the beads you applied previously. Anchor new ones by repeating step one. Butt the beads up against each other; fill in the gaps so that the fabric shade doesn't show.

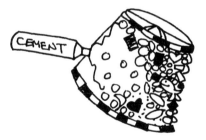

That's all there is to it — keep working 'til it's full. Allow an extra day to dry completely.

Variations:

• Glop on the cement and pour seedbeads over the wet cement. This can give a wonderful pebbly effect.

• Apply your cement in diamond shaped geometric patterns. Add black seedbeads to the lined areas. When it's dry, fill in the diamonds with different colored seedbeads. This looks like stained glass. Also try experimenting with other patterns.

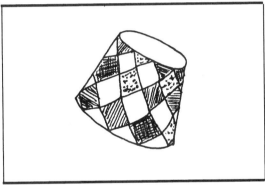

The Tiger Tail Lampshade

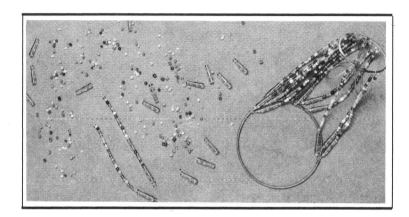

If you're on the go alot and you need a portable project to take with you, this is it.

This lampshade works up in units — you'll make the same segments, then assemble it all at one time. You can carry the segments with you, and work them up in your spare time. Although you can pre-thread your design on the tigertail cable (and work without having to worry about losing beads), in the beginning you may want to work on this one strand at a time.

Supplies Needed:

- Tigertail cable in .018 weight
- Crimp beads
- 1/4" and 3/8" Jump rings (the number is determined by the number of strands you end up with).
- Crimping plier
- Wire cutters
- One standard lampshade frame, with a 3" circumference at the top, and a 5" circumference at the bottom.
- One matte knife
- Appx. ½ kilo (17.6 oz.) of multicolor 4 x 6 mm beads
- 1½" long glass tube accent beads (you will need one per strand, and your final number may vary by the number of strands you end up with in this project. (anywhere between 65 to 90, depending on how full you want the final shade to be).

Step One:

Using the matte knife, cut the fabric plastic liner shade off of the wire lampshade frame. This is actually cheaper than buying the plain frame, plus you will have the loops at the top to attach to your bulb.

Working right from the spool, thread 6" of your smaller beads, then one accent bead.

Step Two:

Add two crimp beads to the end, then make a loop which catches one of your ¼" jumprings. Thread the end of the tigertail back into the two crimp beads and some of your beads.

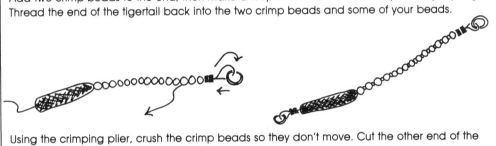

Using the crimping plier, crush the crimp beads so they don't move. Cut the other end of the tigertail about 6" away from the first bead. Add two crimp beads and repeat the crimping process.

Step Three:

Repeat this until you have the desired number of segments to go around to give it a nice, full look. Attach the 1/4" jumpring at each end to 3/8" jumprings, and hook them to the lampshade frame (one end of the fringe to the small loop, and one end to the larger loop, with the longer accent bead at the bottom. Repeat until all of your segments are used.

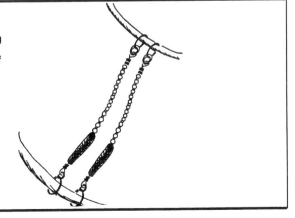

Freeform Woven Lampshade

This lampshade uses a variety of freeform weaving stitches. It's worked on a different style frame — the kind that's usually used for fabric or stained glass.

Because of the large number of beads, the lampshade shown is worked in acrylic crystal — this lacks the fire of true crystal, but it is a lot less expensive. You can work it in almost any round transparent bead to get an "almost stained glass" effect.

You'll work this one panel at a time. Your actual number of beads will vary due to your style of weaving.

Supplies Needed:

- One lampshade frame
- ±330 black 8mm round crystal beads
- ±480 clear 8mm round crystal beads
- ±600 blue 8mm round crystal beads
- ±300 beige 8mm round crystal beads.
- Cement
- One spool of "F" weight silk thread (nylon bead cord will also do)
- One sharps needle (or any needle that will go thru your beads)

Step One:

Work with your thread doubled. Thread your needle, and tie the tail end to the lampshade. Using a looping stitch, start attaching your beads in the illustrated pattern to one panel of the wire frame. (One black, one clear, one black, etc. Continue all the way around the inside of the panel. Pull your thread tightly as you work.

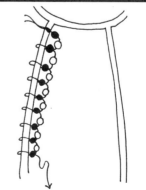

Step Two:

Now bring a line of black beads across the bottom, two-thirds from the top of the panel.

Step Three:

Now you'll add another row of beads using the same stitches. Remember, everything below the black line is to be clear; the blues are at the top, and the beige is in the middle.

Step Four:

Weave down to the bottom (as shown) and add enough clear beads to extend to the center of the black line; go thru one black bead, then add enough clear to match the previous strand, and catch one crystal bead from the perimeter weaving. Most of the stitching on this freeform piece is by making these tangent lines, then filling in with bead-covered thread to fill it up.

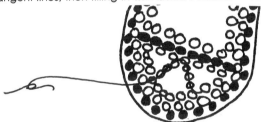

Step Five:

Be creative by making loops or diamond shapes. Bridge the gaps and fill in with beads. Knot and add thread as needed. When you're done with one panel, go on to the next. Cement all knots when done. Middy braid (optional) can be wrapped around the metal frame if desired.

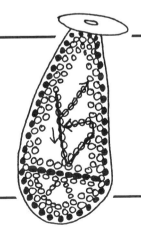

Woven Mesh Lampshade

This is a very quick lampshade to make. You use larger beads, and the pattern is very easy. Whereas some of the other woven patterns are freeform or more offset, this one works up more "rank and file" to give a very definite squared look.

Supplies Needed:

- One lampshade frame with a 3" top circumference, 5" bottom circumference, and appx. 5" height.
- One spool of "F" weight silk thread (nylon bead cord will also do)
- 33 pastel 20 x 10mm oval glass beads
- 22 pastel 20 x 10mm teardrop glass beads
- 132 pastel 8mm round glass beads
- 750 transparent violet size 8 seedbeads
- Cement
- One sharps needle (or any needle that will go thru your beads)

Step One:

Work with your thread doubled. Thread your needle, and make a knot in the tail end of the thread. Stitch thru your lampshade, from inside to out. Add one seedbead, one oval bead, and one seedbead. Stitch back thru your lampshade from outside to inside. Stitch back thru your previous seedbead, add one seedbead, add one oval, one seedbead, and stitch back thru your lampshade. Continue this pattern around. You should have 11 units.

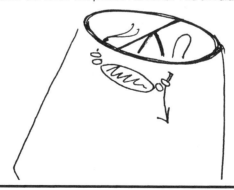

Step Two:

Bring your needle thru the perpendicular seedbead, add 2 seedbeads, 1 round, 4 seedbeads, 1 round, 4 seedbeads, 1 round, and 2 seedbeads. Go thru 1 seedbead, 1 large oval, then 1 seedbead from your previous row. Repeat the pattern.

Fill in the gaps by building on the first part of the row that you beaded and "bridging the gap" with the same design.

Step Three:

For the next row, you'll add 1 seedbead, 1 large oval, 2 seedbeads, 1 large oval, 2 seedbeads, 1 large oval, 1 seedbead. Bring your needle up thru 3 of the 4 seedbeads, 1 round, 3 of 4 seedbeads from your previous row. Repeat.

Fill in the gaps.

Step Four:

The pattern for the next row is 1 seedbead, 1 round, 5 seedbeads, 1 round, 5 seedbeads, 1 round, 1 seedbead. Go thru 1 seedbead, 1 oval, 1 seedbead from previous row. Continue on.

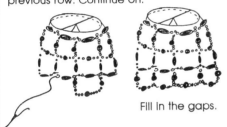

Fill in the gaps.

Step Five:

The next row's pattern is 1 seedbead, 1 teardrop, 6 seedbeads, 1 round, 6 seedbeads, 1 teardrop, 1 seedbead. Repeat.

Add new thread as you work by weaving in your old ends, and adding new. Reinforce with knots and cement.

Step Six:

For the next row, add 1 seedbead, 1 round, 8 seedbeads, 1 round, 8 seedbeads, 1 round, 1 seedbead. Weave as shown.

Step Seven:

For the last row, add 1 seedbead, 1 teardrop, 2 seedbeads, 1 round, 2 seedbeads, 1 round, 2 seedbeads, 1 round, 2 seedbeads, 1 round, 2 seedbeads, 1 teardrop, 1 seedbead. Weave as shown.

Weave in all your ends and cement.

Sewing Machine Lampshade

This one looks so great, yet it works up so easy! You'll prethread your beads, then catch them every so often with the sewing machine. It looks so hard, but it's not!

Supplies Needed:

- One lampshade frame (any size)
- One spool of "F" weight silk thread (nylon bead cord will also do)
- One sharps needle (or any size that fits your beads)
- Appx. ½ kilo (17.6 oz.) of glass beads
- Grosgrain ribbon
- One sewing machine with zigzag capabilities
- 527 Cement

Step One:

Prethread your beads on your thread. Work right from the spool. Do not cut off excess.

Step Two:

With your sewing machine zigzagging, Anchor the end of the thread to the grosgrain ribbon. Slide the desired number of beads down, then zigzag to secure that loop. Continue on.

Step Three:

Cement the finished stitchwork on the grosgrain ribbon to the inside edge of your desired frame.

Comanche Stitch Lampshade

This lampshade is actually several Comanche stitch earrings attached together. You can work them up as a portable craft and take them with you when you're on-the-go. After making the required number of earrings, simply assemble them in a couple of hours into a truly grand lampshade.

They are a combination of stitches, but the most recognized is the Comanche Stitch (also known as the "Brick Stitch") that makes the top part.

When you first look at this lampshade, it may seem a little confusing as to where to start. What you need to do is break it into several steps. It is actually composed of 20 earrings, connected together and attached to the frame.

Supplies Needed:

- 3 hanks each of peach, beige, and light blue seedbeads
- One lampshade frame 5" in diameter
- Nylon bead cord in "D" weight
- English beading needle #10 or 12
- 1" long bugle beads
- One package of "middy" braid
- 527 cement
- Nymo in "0" or "00"
- One sharps needle

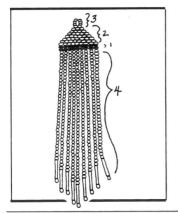

Each earring can be divided into steps.

(1) is the base of the earring. You will start with this section. It is composed of seedbeads. This sets the tone for the earring: the number of beads here will eventually be your number of fringes when you are done.

(2) This is the actual Comanche Stitch. The number of beads decreases with each row.

(3) This is the loop that attaches to the lampshade frame.

(4) This is your fringe.

This is your pattern:

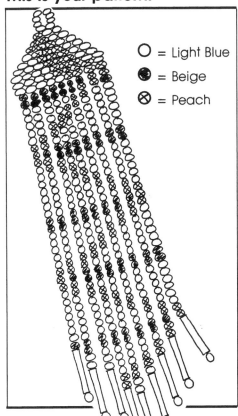

O = Light Blue

◑ = Beige

⊗ = Peach

Step One:

Cut 2 yards of nymo and thread your needle. You'll work single thread. Don't knot the end, leave a 2" tail that you can weave in later. Put four seedbeads on your needle.

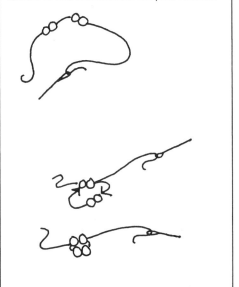

Bring the needle around and enter the same 4 beads again in the same order. As you pull tightly, they'll fall into place "side by side", like 2 little sticks of dynamite.

Step Two:

Reinforce by repeating this two more times. You'll add beads two at a time by repeating this stitch. Keep working until you have your desired width.

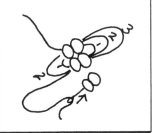

Step Three:

You just completed part (1). Now, on to part (2). This is the true Comanche Stitch. Turn your piece so that the thread is coming out of the right side top. If you are right handed, you will be working from right to left. Add a seedbead to your thread. With your needle, catch the little bundle of threads, go back up thru the seedbead. It is very important that you go thru the bead in the opposite direction than you just did, or the bead will not lay right. The hole should be facing up. If it's facing sideways, you need to re-do that last step.

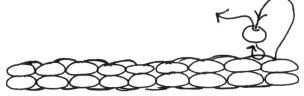

Step Four:

Work across the row. When you get to the end, turn, and continue on across. Because your beadwork is actually building on the spaces between the beads, each row will have one fewer bead in it. Continue until there are two beads in this row. You are now ready to start part (3).

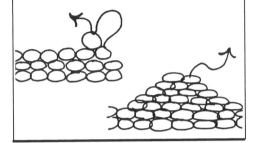

Step Five:

This step is really easy: You're going to make the loop at the top. Think of the last two beads in the top row as "A" and "B". Bring your needle out of "A", add 6 seedbeads, go back down into "B". Repeat this twice to strengthen the loop. This is where the earring attaches to the lampshade frame, and it's best to reinforce.

Step Six:

You just completed part (3). Weave your thread down through the earring to the center row. If you need to add new thread, simply weave in the ends from the first strand, anchor a second strand by weaving in the first end, then you're ready to continue stitching. Fringing is very easy. Start with the center. Bring your thread out of the bottom of the center seedbeads. Add more seedbeads in your design, then a bugle bead, then one seedbead at the bottom to be your pivot bead (see page 12), then back up thru your fringe. This design has the longest fringe in the center, which, when you assemble the lampshade, gives a wonderful rippling effect. Work out in one direction, then back to center, and work out the other way. You can keep better track of your fringe by always working out from the center.

Step Seven:

Weave in all loose threads, and cement if necessary. After making 20 of these, you're ready to assemble your lampshade. Lay out all of your earrings, so that the design alternates right and left with each one. Thread a new long piece of nymo, and tie the tail end to the frame. Work with your thread doubled, in a blanket stitch, attach the earrings to the lampshade frame by catching the top loop. Be aware of the distance between earrings: they should be just touching on the outside edges. When you're done attaching all 20 earrings to the frame, go back and loop the earrings together on the ends by weaving single-strand nymo thru the end rows of beads.

Cover the frame by wrapping with "Middy" braid when done. Cement to secure.

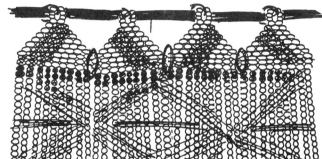

Design your own patterns:

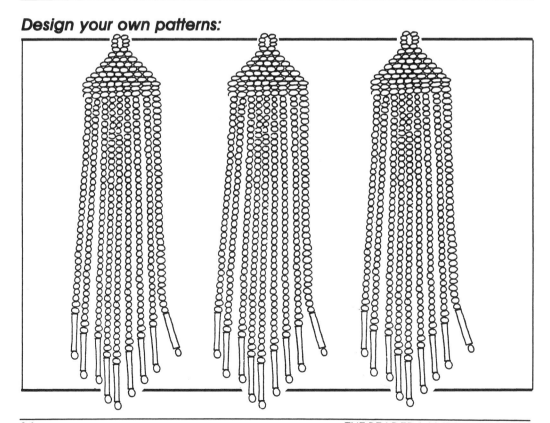

Peyote Stitch Cutout Lampshade

If you like working in Peyote Stitch, this is the project for you! It works up very quickly because you're working with larger glass beads, and the effect is quite stunning!

Use cobalt blue glass with a black lampshade — it has a "magical" effect!

Supplies Needed:

- One square lampshade frame appx. 4" wide at the top, and 9" wide at the bottom (per panel)
- One spool of "F" weight silk thread (nylon bead cord will also do)
- One sharps needle (or any size that fits your beads)
- Appx. 200 glass tube beads, 10 x 3mm
- One matte knife
- Four charms (optional)
- Watchmaker's cement

Step One:

Using a template, cut out a diamond shape in the center of each side of the lampshade.

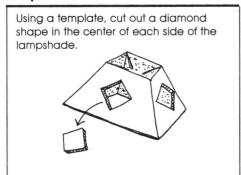

Step Two:

Working with your thread doubled, at the top of the diamond, bring your needle from the inside to the outside (stitch right thru your lampshade. Add enough beads to fill the length, and go back into the bottom part of the diamond (from outside to inside) with your needle.

Step Three:

Bring the needle back thru the lampshade very close to where your last stitch was. Add one glass bead, skip one, go into the next one, add one, skip one, go into the next one, etc. Don't worry if the beads start to offset — that's the normal Peyote pattern.

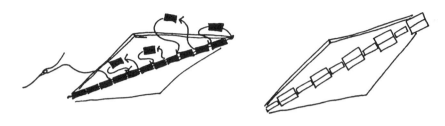

Step Four:

When you get to the top, once again secure your thread by passing thru the lampshade; bring the needle back out, and continue weaving in the same pattern. Work until the hole is filled with glass beads. You can even dangle a moon or star charm from the bottom. Continue on until all 4 sides are done. Cement and knot as needed.

Varations:

Instead of using the Peyote stitch, try using the Satin stitch to quickly fill the opening.

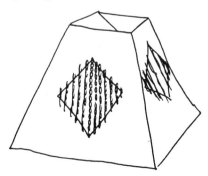 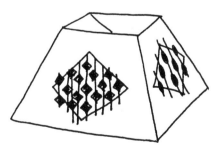

Try other weaving stitches for special effects, or use large geometric beads that create a pattern as they fit together.

Crystal & Wire Lampshade

If you like the look of crystal, and want to make a REALLY easy lampshade, then this is for you!

You don't need a needle, all you'll do is wirebend this into shape! . . . and, best of all, it's quick (you can finish it in one afternoon).

Supplies Needed:

- One dome lampshade frame with a long finial (top)
- One spool of 24 gauge silver-colored beading wire
- 252 8mm AB crystal
- 48 10x8mm fuschia crystal
- 217 6mm gyro cut fuschia crystal
- 13 24x21mm side drilled AB teardrop crystal
- 13 star-shaped napkin rings
- One wire cutter

Step One:

Thread your crystal onto your wire in an alternating pattern (1 AB, 1 fuschia, etc.) Take 12 (6 of each) and bend into a ring. Secure (twist) and trim wire.

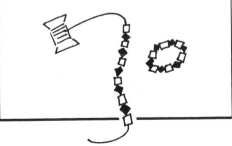

Step Two:

Take the long crystal-covered length of wire from the spool. Make a large ring of 204 beads, and secure. Bend into a "flower" shape with 6 petals.

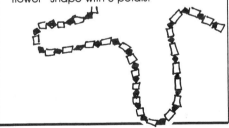

Step Three:

Hook a new piece of crystal-covered wire and secure one end to the small ring. Slide 7 beads down, catch the second ring at the center of one of your "petals", and loop the wire around. Slide down 21 beads (including 4 teardrop fuschia (see diagram), then clip wire about 2" away from the last bead.

Step Four:

Add your napkin ring, and wire bend a loop to connect.

Step Five:

Wirebend a bail for your side-drilled crystal, add one fuschia, and connect to the loop you just made in the napkin ring.

Step Six:

The next strand you attach will be between "petals". You'll alternate positions to have a total of 12 "fringes" hanging down.

Wirebend a 13th crystal and napkin ring combination, and attach to the top of the finial with the wire.

African Woven Lampshade

This is a very natural, wonderful type of lampshade. You'll embellish a storebought shade. The beads are not meant to be transparent, rather, they have an earthy quality. Use a tan shade and clay lamp to carry through with the design.

It's best to work this directly onto the shade, to keep its shape.

Supplies Needed:

- One spool of "F" weight nylon bead cord.
- One sharps needle
- 9 Ashantis or Akubas (brass charms from Africa which depict women, faces, animals, etc.
- 700 Size 6 striped seedbeads ("E-Beads") (This includes extras)
- African Trade Beads:
  — 72 thinner tube beads ("A")
  — 18 2" long wider beads ("B")
  — 45 1" long wider beads ("C")
- One flaired lampshade
- Cement

Step One:

Thread your needle with 6' of thread. Work with thread doubled. Add 45 E beads, tie ends together to form a loop. Go back thru to reinforce.

Step Two:

String on 11 E beads, skip 4 in your ring, bring your needle thru the 5th. Add 11 more, skip 4, go into the 5th in your ring. Repeat all the way around. You should have 9 loops.

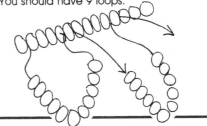

Step Three:

Bring your needle to the 6th E bead in your loop (the center). Add 5 E beads, 1 "A" trade bead, 5 more E beads. Bring your needle thru the 6th bead in the next loop. Continue on in this pattern.

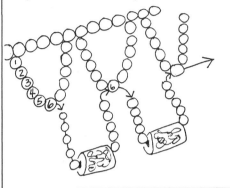

Step Four:

At this point, you can stitch your A trade beads to the top of the shade. If you need to add extra thread, knot and weave in your ends, then add new thread by weaving in.

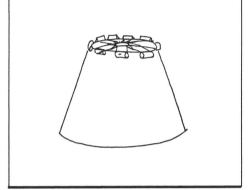

Step Five:

Weave your way down thru the "A" bead. Add 5 E beads, 1 C trade bead, 5 E beads, 1 A trade bead, 5 E beads, 1 C trade bead, 5 E beads. Bring your needle thru the next A bead from the previous row. Repeat the pattern.

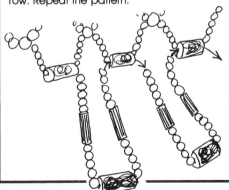

Step Six:

Bring your needle down to the next A bead from this newest row. Add 5 E beads, 1 B, 5 E, and back thru that previous row's A. Repeat around.

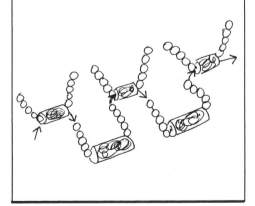

Step Seven:

Repeat the same pattern as the previous row, but instead of adding B trade beads, use A again. Add thread as needed.

Step Eight:

Repeat Step Five.

Step Nine:

Repeat Step Eight.

Step Ten:

Add 5 E, 1 C, 5 E, 1 B, 5 E, add one Ashanti, add 5 E, back up thru your last B (Whereas the others have been horizontal, this one is now vertical.) Continue around. You're almost done!

Cement your knots and weave in your ends.

The Diamond Stitch Lampshade

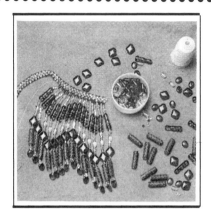

Sometimes you'll be beading onto a ribbon as a base, but with this lampshade, you'll create your own base with the diamond stitch.

This gives you the freedom to adjust your pattern as needed; if the lampshade is wider, you can add on. If it's narrower, then you decrease your number of fringe. You can even go back later (after you'd thought you were finished) and add on. It's very versatile!

To help grip as you work, use a clipboard.

Supplies Needed:

- Nylon bead cord in "F" weight
- One sharps needle
- Crystal & red "E" beads (the amount is determined by your circumference).
- Red glass tube beads
- Clear 7x10mm glass oval beads
- Enhancing beads (I've used metal beads that are studded with glass dots)
- Cement
- One large eyed needle
- Red oval glass beads
- Red diamond-shaped flat glass beads
- One lampshade

Step One:

Using your sharps needle and your crystal "E" beads, you'll start with your diamond stitch to create your base.

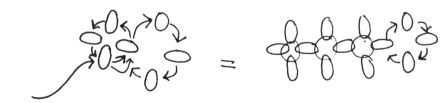

Step Two:

You'll then want to fill in with your red beads.

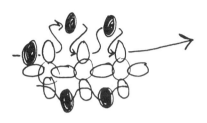

Step Three:

Now that you have your base, you're ready to start your fringe. This uses one of the techniques for fringing shown on page 12.

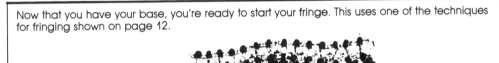

That's really all there is to it!

Art Deco Lampshade

To make this stunning lampshade, you'll start off by working your stitches onto a grosgrain ribbon. You'll first measure circumference (please see page 19), and use a grosgrain ribbon a few inches longer (so that you can foldover and stitch, to eliminate fraying.

I find it easier to tape my ribbon onto a piece of shelving that is portable. Then you can either write your measurements right onto the ribbon (marking where your fringes go), or tape a tape measure or graph paper next to it for reference. The actual stitching is very easy and relaxing (like handwork), and as long as your shelving is not too heavy, it's easy to take with when you're on the go. For smaller lampshades, you can even tape it to a box lid or clipboard as you work.

Supplies Needed:

- One lampshade (I like the look of black metal with this)
- 104 7x10mm rectangle black fire polished crystal
- 91 7x10mm clear (or AB) fire polished crystal
- 104 4mm round clear (or AB)fire polished crystal
- 78 6mm black round fire polished crystal
- 13 14x10mm black teardrop fire polished crystal
- 1 hank size 9° hematite color seedbeads
- 1 hank milky white size 11° seedbeads
- Cement
- One spool of "F" weight nymo thread (nylon bead cord will also do)
- One size 10 English beading needle
- 527 Cement
- Appx. 1½ yards 1/8" wide grosgrain ribbon (beige is good)

Step One:

Divide your circumference by 13. This tells you where to place your loops. Write right on the grosgrain. Tape the ends down on your shelf. You have 13 repeating units. Then, divide up each unit by the number of places you'll need to stitch (each loop has 2).

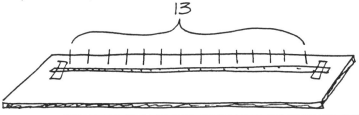

13

Step Two:

Working with your thread doubled, stitch into the grosgrain (make a knot in the end), then a couple of staystitches to lock in that end so it doesn't come loose. Start with your outermost fringe in the first unit. Add 8 white seedbeads, 1 hematite seedbead, 7 seedbeads, 1 4mm round, 7 seedbeads, 1 black rect., 7 seedbeads, 1 clear rect., 7 seedbeads, 1 round black, 3 seedbeads, 1 round black, 3 seedbeads, 1 round black, 7 seedbeads, 1 clear rect. crystal, 7 seedbeads, 1 black rect. crystal, 7 seedbeads, 1 4mm crystal, 1 hematite seedbead, 8 seedbeads. Staystitch.

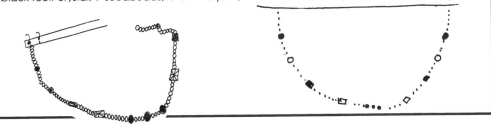

Step Three:

Move over to your next mark. Add 7 seedbeads, 1 hematite, 7 seedbeads, 1 clear round, 3 seedbeads, 1 black rect., 5 seedbeads, 1 clear rect., 4 seedbeads, 1 black round, 3 seedbeads, 1 black round, 4 seedbeads, 1 clear rect., 5 seedbeads, 1 black rect., 3 seedbeads, 1 clear round, 7 seedbeads, 1 hematite, 7 seedbeads. Staystitch.

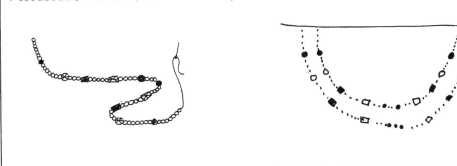

Step Four:

Move over to your next mark. Add 7 seedbeads, 1 hematite, 7 seedbeads, 1 clear round, 3 seedbeads, 1 black rect., 3 seedbeads, 1 clear rect., 3 seedbeads, 1 black round, 3 seedbeads, 1 clear rect., 3 seedbeads, 1 black rect., 3 seedbeads, 1 clear round, 7 seedbeads, 1 hematite, 7 seedbeads. Staystitch.

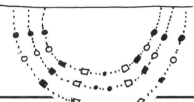

Step Five:

Move over to your next mark. Add 7 seedbeads, 1 hematite, 7 seedbeads, 1 clear round, 3 seedbeads, 1 black rect., 3 seedbeads, 1 clear rect., 3 seedbeads, 1 black rect., 3 seedbeads, 1 clear round, 7 seedbeads, 1 hematite, 7 seedbeads. Staystitch.

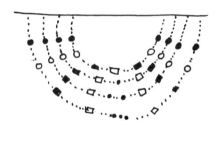

Step Six:

Move over to your next mark (the center of your unit). Add 7 seedbeads, 1 hematite, 2 seedbeads, down thru your black teardrop, 1 seedbead, back up thru your teardrop, 2 seedbeads, 1 hematite, 7 seedbeads, and staystitch.

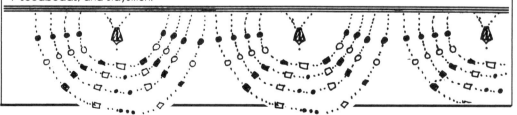

Repeat as needed. When done, use your 527 to adhere the grosgrain to the inside of your shade. Position to show your fringe. Allow a day to dry.

The Turkish Lampshade

This lamp was truly a find. It's made of brass, and has such a distinctive look to it, that it's quite wonderful! Many thanks to my friend, Anna, who let me borrow it back to photograph after she got it from me. Sorry it took so long, Anna!

Supplies Needed:

- "D" weight nymo
- One size 10 English beading needle
- Red size 11° seedbeads
- Aqua size 5 bugle beads
- A mixture of size 11° seedbeads
- Cement

Your Pattern:

This is just your basic fringing technique worked on grosgrain ribbon. Measure as previously explained. Work your fringe one at a time (see diagram), and stitch or cement to your lampshade. That's all there is to it!

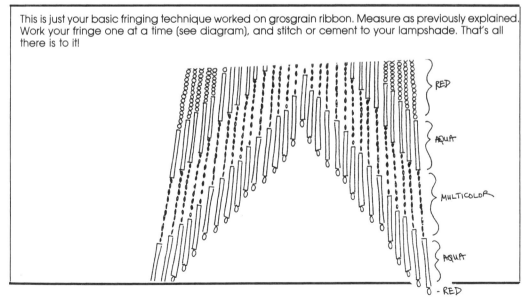

RED

AQUA

MULTICOLOR

AQUA

O - RED

The secret to this beautiful lampshade is to weave your fringes just the right distance apart, so that your design shows to its best advantage. If you weave too close, it will appear crowded; to far apart, your design will be lost. If you need to adjust this to fit your shade, I suggest leaving your fringes the same distance apart where your design is, and just add to subtract in an area that doesn't have a design.

All you need is one, maybe two, repeats of the butterfly, and inbetween, you can have just the top and bottom borders repeat. Please see the diagram on the following page for the pattern. Below is the color key.

You work this lampshade by stitching into your grosgrain (see previous instructions), and stitch at about 1/8 to 1/16" intervals to achieve the best effects.

Supplies Needed:
- Nymo in "D" or "F" weight
- One #10 or 12 English beading needle
- 1¼" long satin bugle beads
- Cement
- Seedbeads in the following colors: fuschia, violet, aqua, bronze, rootbeer, rose, yellow, lt. blue, peridot, and LOTS of white.
- One lampshade

Step One:

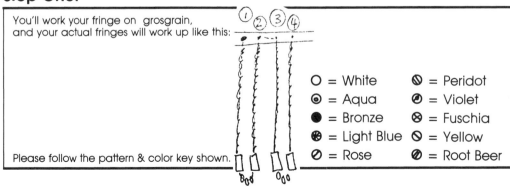

You'll work your fringe on grosgrain, and your actual fringes will work up like this:

Please follow the pattern & color key shown.

O = White	◐ = Peridot
◉ = Aqua	◑ = Violet
● = Bronze	⊗ = Fuschia
✳ = Light Blue	◒ = Yellow
⊘ = Rose	⊘ = Root Beer

Graph paper for your own fringe designs.

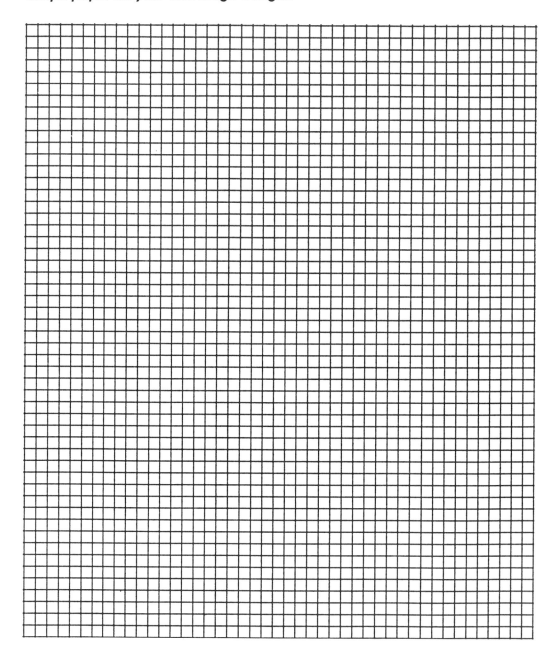

THE BEADED LAMPSHADE BOOK

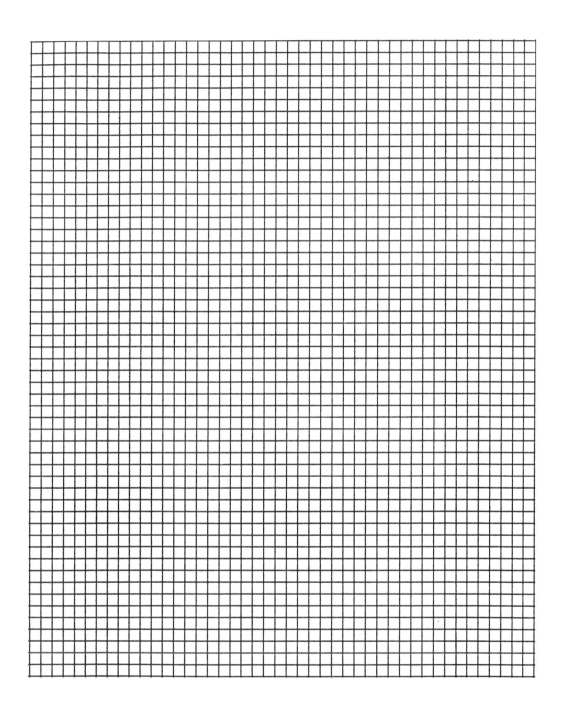

INTERSTELLAR

TRADING & PUBLISHING COMPANY

If you'd like a list of other titles and forthcoming books
from the INTERSTELLAR TRADING & PUBLISHING COMPANY,
please send a stamped-self addressed envelope to:

**THE INTERSTELLAR TRADING & PUBLISHING COMPANY
POST OFFICE BOX 2215
LA MESA, CALIFORNIA 91943**